# The Best Beach Day Ever

by Alix Wood

> Every care has been taken to ensure the safety of these activities. There is an element of risk in any activity and therefore it is important that children are supervised by a responsible adult.

First published 2012 by Truran, an imprint of Tor Mark, United Downs Ind Est, Redruth, Cornwall TR16 5HY

www.truranbooks.co.uk

ISBN 978 185022 239 2

Printed and bound in Cornwall by
R Booth Ltd, The Praze, Penryn TR10 8AA

# Contents

# Planning your day

What should you take? What should you leave behind? How do you choose your beach? What should you check before you go?

## Essentials

- Sunscreen
- Towels x 2 each
- Bathing suits
- Sunglasses
- Hats
- Rubbish bags
- Flip flops or similar

## For a young family

- Fishing nets
- Bucket and spade
- Pens and paper
- Beach umbrella or tent
- Arm bands or swimming aids
- Plasters and anti-bacterial wipes
- First aid kit

## For older children

- Magazines or books
- Music player and earphones
- Surf boards, wet suits, rash vest
- Tennis ball or beach ball

## Dogs

- Water and a bowl
- Poo bags

## Useful

- After-sun cream
- Cool box and a picnic
- Windbreak and chairs

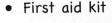

Sun screen

## Useful car kit

It is useful to have a few extra things in the car for when you get back. A large bin liner or two for sandy surfboards and wetsuits. A couple of spare towels for wet bottoms to sit on. A hot flask of tea can be very welcome. A soft dustpan brush is great for brushing down sandy people before they get in the car.

## Check it still fits

Don't forget to try on your bathing costumes and wetsuits before you go!

## What NOT to take

Only take things that you wouldn't mind losing. Thieves often target beaches and beach car parks.

- Valuables
- Expensive cameras and mobile phones
- Passports etc
- Lilos and inflatables

Only use inflatables in swimming pools. They can float out to sea on even the calmest day. Don't risk it.

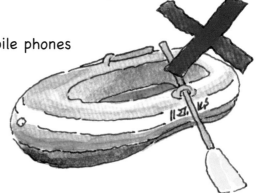

5

## Find your beach

Choose a beach that will suit your family and what
you want to do. Check if it is sandy or pebbly. Is it
deeply shelving or shallow and safer for little ones?
Check if there are lifeguards and whether you will
need toilets, food and drink, surf
board hire and so on. Is it a
good surf beach? Has it got
big waves for surfing or is
it calm for swimming?
Some of that will depend
on the weather of
course! See the inside
back cover for details
of beach guide books
that can help you.

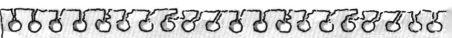

## Check the tide times

Check the times for high and low tide if you want to
explore your beach. Tides come in very
fast and you can easily get cut off while
exploring. An hour or two either side of
low tide is the best time for rock pooling
and looking around. Tide table books can
be found in local shops, or look at the
information boards or ask a lifeguard.
Keep a lookout for the tide's direction
and be aware of how fast the water
is coming in, especially if you're
playing in rock pools.

## Keeping your stuff safe

Leave valuable items at home
if you can, so they don't get
lost or damaged. Maybe use
an inexpensive disposable
camera instead. If you must
take them, put phones, iPods,
cameras, etc. in airtight plastic
bags. Sand can still get inside
their cases. Make sure
someone is always watching
your stuff if you choose to go for a walk
or a swim. A crowded beach is an ideal place for thieves.

## Parking

Make sure you have coins for the car parks, as shops may
refuse to give out change. Get there early, car parks near
the beach often fill up quickly. Take care if you park on the
beach. The tide may come in and wash your car away. Look
out for information boards, and for the high tide mark on
the beach (the line of washed up seaweed). Don't park below
it! Keep valuables out of sight. Never leave
children or pets in a hot car.

# Perfect beach food

Food can make a day out expensive. It is cheaper and fun to take your own. And you know everyone will have something they like.

## Picnic ideas

- Spreads and dips with crusty bread
- Marinated vegetables
- Sandwiches or wraps
- Fried or baked chicken pieces
- Brie or camembert, both of which taste nicer warm, with French bread or biscuits
- Quiche
- Pasta and rice salads
- Potato salad or coleslaw
- Sliced meats like salami, ham or prosciutto
- Sausage rolls
- Mini Cornish pasties
- Fruit salad or fruit
- Cakes and biscuits
- Yoghurts
- Cold drinks - freeze them the night before

### Useful Picnic Things
Picnic food and drinks
Picnic basket or cooler
Plastic cutlery & napkins
Corkscrew
Bottle opener
Hand wipes
Plastic serving utensils
Drinks cooler
Picnic blanket or sheet
Beach chairs
Tin foil

## Food Safety

Most refrigerated foods should be eaten within an hour or two. Take food out at the last moment, and put in a cool bag or box. Frozen plastic ice blocks will keep your food cool, or use large bags of ice, and then use the ice in drinks too. Alternatively, freeze small bottles of water or squash to keep the food cool and drink them once they've started to thaw. Keep food out of the sun as much as possible and keep it covered. This protects from insects and gives it some shade. Tin foil is good for covering food as it can be tucked underneath so it won't get blown away.

## No picnic table?

Dig two deep parallel trenches in moist sand for everyone's legs. The area in between is the table. Lay a clean towel over it, and hey presto - comfortable dining!

## DON'T feed the gulls!

Don't be tempted to feed the seagulls. Most coastal areas have problems with gulls. If they get used to scavenging food they will swoop and snatch food from people. This can be scary for young children. Make sure you dispose of food properly. Be warned - some areas will fine people for feeding gulls.

9

## Useful Barbecue Things

- Food to cook!
- Matches or lighter
- Firelighters
- Tin foil
- Rubbish bags
- Utensils
- Cooking oil and brush
- Bucket for sand or water
- Sauces and salad dressings

## Barbecue Food

Try fish, steaks, burgers, vegetables and kebabs. Cheap sausages never cook as well, try and get some with a high meat content. Don't forget salads and breads. For the vegetables, jacket potatoes and corn cobs wrapped in foil are classics. Pre-cook the potatoes in a microwave if using a disposable barbecue as it won't stay hot long enough. Try covering the corn with a garlic and cayenne mayonnaise and roll it in grated parmesan. Or try slices of courgette, mushrooms and peppers brushed with oil on a skewer. For pudding, barbecue pineapple slices or try banana with some chocolate placed in a slit in the middle.

## Using disposable barbecues

Light, and then wait until the flames die down and the coals have a layer of greyish white ash on them. Brush the grill with oil to prevent sticking. The centre will generally be hotter. Cook everything at a good temperature and for long enough. Nothing spoils your summer like food poisoning!

## Barbecue safety

- Check barbecues are allowed on the beach
- Choose a level, sheltered site, away from people and flammable things
- Don't put a barbecue on dry leaves, grass or wood. Soil or sand is safer
- Have a bucket of water or sand close by in case
- Keep children and pets away
- Never leave a barbecue unattended
- Never light a barbecue indoors or in a tent
- Do not wear loose clothing, especially long sleeves
- Keep matches and lighters well away from children

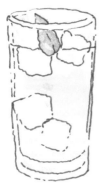

## Home made lemonade

Put the juice of 6 fresh lemons and 150g caster sugar into a big jug and add 2 mugs of boiling water. Stir until all of the sugar has dissolved. Add 600ml cold water and mix. Pour into bottles, put the lids on and leave them in the fridge overnight.

## Packing up

Let the barbecue cool down. Pour water on it and on the sand underneath – sand keeps its heat and can still burn someone's feet after 2 hours! Never put hot ashes in a bin. Take the remains home by wrapping it in tin foil once it is cool enough. You can put the cold charcoal in the compost bin and the mesh and aluminium tray in the recycling.

# Getting settled

**Where should you pitch camp? How can you find your family on a crowded beach or escape the hot sun?**

### Where to pitch camp?

There are two main things to consider — safety and not having to keep moving camp. For safety, make sure you are not under any cliffs. Rockfalls can occur and will happen very suddenly. Just because there are no signs of rockfall doesn't mean there wont be a fresh one right where you are sitting. Don't risk it! Check the beach for any broken glass or hot spots from barbecues. Try and chose a nice flat bit, and look where the tide line is (where all the driftwood and seaweed forms a line at high tide). You want to be further up the beach than that or you'll have to keep moving as the tide comes in.

Keep radio volume low. Noise travels on the beach and you don't want to upset your neighbours.

## Signpost
On a crowded beach it's a good idea to make a flag so you can all find your pitch easily.

## Phone signal
Most beaches I've been to do not have a phone signal. Don't rely on getting one in an emergency. Higher ground improves your chances.

## Sand manners
Avoid walking too close to other people's towels while wearing flip flops. It will flip the sand right onto their towel.

## Umbrella skills
If you have a beach umbrella (and want to keep it!) put it in the sand at an angle, and so the wind blows against the umbrella, not underneath it.

## Make a beach shelter!
Too hot? Dig a trench large enough to lie down in and build up 3 walls around it. Make sure the sand forming the walls is compacted enough and then drape a towel across the walls (or a surfboard). Weigh the towel down either side with some stones.

# Keeping safe

It's important to know what to do to keep your family safe. Beaches are fun, but there are dangers you need to be aware of.

## Important sea safety

- Read the safety signs at the beach. They help you identify hazards and find the safest areas to swim. They also have the information you can give to emergency services to help them locate you quickly in an emergency
- Never swim alone
- Swim between the red and yellow striped flags
- If you get into trouble in the sea, stick your hand in the air and shout for help
- If you see someone in trouble, tell a lifeguard
- If you can't see a lifeguard, call 999 or 112 and ask for the coastguard

- Don't use inflatables. Even a slight breeze can sweep you out to sea
- Keep an eye on children at all times and agree on a meeting point when you arrive at the beach in case you are separated
- Don't go into the sea after drinking alcohol. It slows your reactions and can impair your ability to judge distances

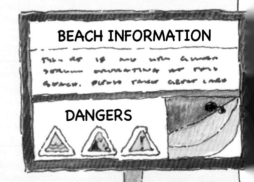

BEACH INFORMATION

DANGERS

# Know your flags

On beaches patrolled by lifeguards, different flags tell you where it's safest to swim and which areas are designated for water sports.

 The area between the red-and-yellow flags is patrolled by lifeguards. This is the safest place to swim and bodyboard

 The area between black-and-white chequered flags is the area for water sports like surfing and kayaking. Never swim or bodyboard here

 The red flag indicates that it is dangerous to swim or get in the water. Never go in the water when the red flag is flying

 The orange windsock means there are offshore winds. Never use an inflatable when you see the sock flying as the wind could push you offshore very quickly

# Sun safety

To have a great day, you don't want sunburn. Make sure you put sunscreen on those easily forgotten areas like the tops of feet, ears and the back of the neck. Use sunscreen with an SPF of 15 or more and which protects against UVA and UVB rays. Two tablespoons of sun cream should cover all your exposed skin, if you're wearing a swimsuit. Re-apply every two hours even if it's labelled waterproof. Wear a hat and sunglasses with a CE Mark, a UV 400 label and 100% UV protection.

# Watch out for...

## Rip currents

The most common incidents lifeguards deal with involve rip currents that quickly take paddling children, bodyboarders and swimmers out of their depth. Rips can occur at any beach with waves. Safe waves come all the way in to the shore in straight lines. Signs of a rip are gaps in the waves, brown sandy water, foam on the water's surface and debris floating out to sea. Lifeguards know their beaches and are experienced in spotting them. The red and yellow flags show the safest areas to swim. Ideally, have your beach day at a lifeguard patrolled beach.

### What to do if you are caught in a rip

Stay calm. If you can stand, wade ashore, don't swim. Keep hold of your board if you have one to help you float. Raise your hand and shout for help. Never try to swim directly against the rip. It's stronger than you and you'll get exhausted. Swim parallel to the beach until free of the rip, then make for shore.

Green arrows - escape routes

## Weever fish and Jellyfish stings

When paddling, wear flip flops. Weever fish hide in the sand and have venomous spines on their backs. If you step on one, the sting is painful. Place the stung area in hot water. Test the water first so you don't scald the person too! If stung by a jellyfish, do not rub the area as this makes the pain worse. Lightly spray the area with seawater and apply a cold compress or ice if available. Seek medical help immediately if you start to feel unwell. You may have an allergic reaction.

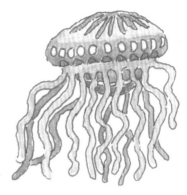

## Tombstoning

Many people have been seriously hurt or killed by jumping from rocks into water. DON'T DO IT! Water depth changes with the tide – it may be shallower than you think. Rocks and submerged objects may not be visible. The shock from the cold water makes it difficult to swim and strong currents could sweep you away. It's not called tombstoning for nothing.

## Dumping waves

A small wave can knock a child over. Dumping waves break with great force in shallow water and occur during low tide.

## Tides

Keep a lookout for the tide's direction and be aware of how fast it is coming in, especially if you're playing in rock pools.

# Fun on the sand

Here are lots of simple games you can play on the sand. A ball and a bucket and spade may come in handy.

### Noughts and crosses toss

Draw a board in the sand and use stones or shells as the counters. The first player tosses a stone at the board. If it lands within a square, leave it on the board. If it is on the lines or off the board, take the stone away and the next players has a turn. Just like noughts and crosses, the object is to be the first one to finish a line of three pebbles.

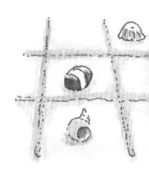

### Scary feet!

Make giant monster footprints that go along the beach.

## TRY THIS!

One person buries some numbered pieces of paper in a square marked out in the sand. The larger the number, the deeper you bury them in the sand. Then everyone races to dig them up again. The highest score wins. You could use shells instead, mussels could be 5 points and limpets, 10 points.

## The Beach Boys

Make music on the beach using popping seaweed, clashing shells and banging driftwood as your instruments.

> Encourage game playing away from other people. It can be very annoying to have people playing ball over your head if you are trying to relax!

## Mr Sandman

Build a snowman out of sand. Feather arms, shell nose, sunhat and sunglasses and seaweed hair perhaps?

## Pebble tower

Collect pebbles of various sizes and see who can build the tallest tower. The flatter and bigger the pebble, the better. If you build a really tall tower, take it down before you leave. It could hurt a little child if it fell.

## Pebble Bowls

Collect two pebbles for each player. Make sure you can recognise yours. Get a smaller distinct pebble to act as the target. Toss the small pebble a good distance, then see who gets the closest with their pebbles. Don't throw near people!

## Scavenger hunt

Give each person a plastic bag and a list of things to find. The first one home with the most items wins. It's a good idea to include a 'longest' or 'smallest' to make sure there is a clear winner.

Perhaps a feather, the longest piece of sea weed, a stone with a stripe in it, a dogfish egg case, a mussel shell, a fossil, a piece of rope, a cuttle fish and some driftwood.

## TRY THIS!

Draw the items instead for a toddler scavenger hunt

## Coin on Coin

Get a bucket full of sea water. Drop a coin to the bottom, then drop a second coin and try and get the second to land on the first. Whoever covers the coin the best wins.

## French Cricket

You will need a bat or tennis racket and a tennis ball. Players stand in a circle, and someone is chosen to bat. The batsman stands with feet together, defending the stumps — his legs below the knee. The other players bowl at the stumps and the batsman must hit the ball away. If a bowler hits the stumps, the batsman is out. If the batsman hits the ball, he can move his feet and turn around to face in another direction. If he doesn't hit the ball, he must try to defend the stumps without moving his feet. You are out if one of the players in the circle catches a hit before it bounces. The player who bowled or caught him out takes the bat.

## Pebble and spoon race

Balance a round pebble on a spoon and see who can run the furthest without it rolling off.

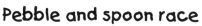

## Knucklebones

Throw up a handful of small pebbles and see how many you can catch on the back of your hand.

## Make a target

Create concentric circles out of sticks or pebbles, or draw them in the sand. Toss a stone from a distance and see who scores a bull's eye.

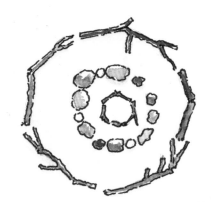

### Snail Croquet

Find a stick and a round pebble. Make a spiral in the sand with the stick. Aim to hit the pebble from the opening to the centre without going over the line on to the other track. If the pebble goes over line, you have to start again.

### Beach shipwreck

Build some islands out of sand, with shark infested sea in between. Players have to jump from one island to the other without falling in the sea. Move the islands further apart if it is too easy.

### Seaweed hairdressers

Collect a pile of seaweed. The cleanest will be closest to the sea as it will have been washed by the waves recently. Take it in turns to give each other elaborate hairstyles, plaits and all. Great fun particularly for balding dads. Wash your hands and head afterwards!

## Beach Bowling

All you need is a ball and a paper cup. Fill the cup with slightly damp sand and turn upside down to make the skittles. Make them in a triangle shape. Then bowl your ball at your handmade skittles. You could create two 'alleys' and race to see who can get them all down.

## Digging

Dig a hole and try to fill it up with water! Or dig a car to drive. Make sure the hole is not too big in case it collapses on you. It can be very dangerous. NEVER dig a tunnel. If you dig a big hole please fill it in before you leave.

# TRY THIS!

Balance limpet shells upside down on your outstretched forefingers, or on your nose. Have races and see who can finish first without dropping their limpet. Make sure the route is clear of obstacles for the nose-balancing version. You can't look down!

## Mystery burial

Bury an object in the sand. Others have to guess what it is from the shape.

## Number Splash

Write numbers on bits of paper. If there are 5 people, write 1-5. Or scratch the numbers on pebbles. Put the numbers in a bag. One player picks out a number and remembers it. He fills a cup or bucket with water and stands in the centre of a circle of the other players. He faces each player in turn, who must say a number between 1 and 5. They must each say a different one. If someone chooses his number, he throws the water at them! If no one does, he has to throw the water over himself! Keep the card somewhere safe so you can check there's no cheating!

### 3 man cricket

A game of cricket usually needs lots of fielders, but you can play on a beach with just a bowler, batsman and wicket keeper. Mark out large circles in the 'field' and if the ball lands in them the batsman is caught out. You can name the 'catchers' and keep a score if you like!

## Dodge Ball

One or two players are the taggers. The taggers must touch the others on the legs with a ball. If someone is tagged they must sit down, but they also join the taggers team, and can tag if they are thrown the ball. You can tag by touching or throwing the ball at the legs. Once everyone is tagged, choose new taggers.

### TRY THIS!

Collect beautiful stones and make a pebble picture on the sand. Take a photo of it to take home.

**Always leave the pebbles on the beach.**

## Hopscotch

Revive the game of hopscotch! Draw out a court with a stick in the sand. If you've forgotten the rules here they are. Toss a marker into the first square. It must land completely within the square. The player hops through the court beginning on square one. Straddle side by side squares. Single squares are hopped on one foot. When you reach the end of the court, turn round and hop back, stopping to pick up the marker on the way. If successful, move to square number two. If the player throws to the wrong square, steps on a line, misses a square, or loses balance, the turn ends. The first player to complete one to ten wins the game.

## Plastic bag kite

All you need is a plastic bag, two sticks and a length of string. Tie the sticks in a cross shape firmly, as shown. Tie a corner of the bag to each end of the cross. Tie a long bit of string to the centre of the cross, and there you have your simple kite. If you run fast and drag it along behind you it should lift into the air.

## Throw it Backwards

Line up side by side, with one person standing about four feet in front, with their back to all the other players. They throw a ball backwards over their head. If the ball is caught, the catcher is the new thrower. If it's caught after a bounce, the catcher hides it behind their back. Everyone puts their hands behind their backs and the thrower must guess who has the ball. If they guess right, they throw again; if not, the person with the ball is the new thrower.

## TRY THIS!

One person makes a trail for the others to follow. Perhaps bury some treasure at the end, or have the picnic lunch set up there. A simple trail can be made by dropping pebbles on the sand or drawing arrows with a stick.

You could make some signs using stones like this.

Turn left          Turn right

## Long John Silver's Treasure

Get an ice cream tub and fill it with 'treasure'; shells, copper coins, pretty pebbles, anything not living. One person buries the tub in the sand while the others aren't looking, (with a discreet marker stone or feather on top so you can find it again if the map fails!). Draw a map with a stick in the sand for the others to use. See who can find Long John Silver's treasure first.

## Jumping race

Draw lines in the sand and see who can jump the furthest.

## Sand Sculpture

It's easiest with really wet, compact sand. To sculpt, make a flat wet sand base, then build up a mound of compacted wet sand, built up out of piles of burger shaped 'sand patties' Then carve away to create your shape. Try making a giant's head in the sand, or a car. Beefburgers and hot dogs are quite easy, make the lettuce and meat from different coloured seaweed.

# Fun in the sea

There are lots of fun things you can do in the sea. Here are some ideas to keep the whole family happy.

## Create your own river

Dig a channel to the sea when the tide is coming in. This should fill with water as the waves will fill any lower land first. You have created your own river! Try making a dam using pebbles and sand. You can make islands, and little bridges. It will all wash away as the tide comes in though. Work fast!

## TRY THIS!

Try making a small raft out of beach finds. Tie some driftwood together with seaweed or rope. Sail your raft in the shallows. Have races on the waves and see whose raft comes in the furthest up the beach.

## Newspaper Boat

1. To make the boat, take a sheet of newspaper and fold a page in half, mark the middle and then with the fold at the top, fold down each side to make equal triangles.

2. Fold half the bottom strip upward on the dotted line.

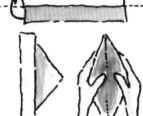

3. Turn the paper over and fold the other lower strip upwards. You now have a paper hat.

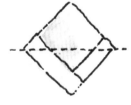

4. Turn it and open it so you're looking inside the part you would wear on your head. The thumbs must be inside.

5. Lay the upper and the lower parts on each other so it looks like a diamond.

6. Fold the lower front triangle upwards along the dotted line. Turn the paper over and fold the other triangle up.

7. Open the hat again and flatten to make a diamond shape again. Pull the upper corners of the triangles in the direction of the arrows. Pull these corners and you'll see the boat forming before your eyes. Stretch the boat both to the right and left, and then separate it slightly from underneath so it can float.

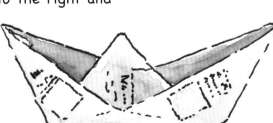

## Stone Skimming

Find a smooth, oval stone the size of the palm of your hand. It should be heavy enough not to get blown about, but light enough that you can throw it accurately. Calm water works best. Throw so the stone hits the water at the flattest possible angle, but ideally with the front side slightly higher than the rear. The best way is to throw the stone from a little above ankle height. Throw it fast with a good amount of spin. Get this with a flick of the wrist at the moment of release. Obviously don't throw near anyone in the water!

## TRY THIS!

To play squirtball you need two beach balls and two water pistols or plastic water bottles with nozzle lids. Draw two goals in the sand. The players try to squirt the beach ball into the opposing player's goal, while guarding their own goal. The stronger the water jets, the better this game works. Enormous water guns work best if you have them. Don't squirt at people!

## Fill the bucket

Split into two teams. Each team has a cup and a bucket. Put both the buckets on the starting line. The first team member on each team rushes to the sea, fills their cups and races back to fill their buckets. Then the next members go in relay. The first full bucket wins.

# Seaside spa pamper day

## Foot spa

Walk to the water's edge, and let the sea water massage your feet. Walk out until the water reaches up to your thighs. Lifting your legs with each stride is tiring, but it's great exercise. There are

beauty benefits, too. Sand is an exfoliant and will give you wonderful soft feet. Seawater contains minerals (iodine and sodium) that help prevent ageing too – and it's so relaxing!

## Dry sand workout

Massage your soles walking on the beach. Wet sand is quite easy. Dry sand is unstable and the shape shifts as you walk, which involves more effort and gives a great foot workout.

## Sea massage

Soak and soothe those aching bones with a relaxing sea massage! Sit in the water and let the waves massage your back. Change positions forward, backwards or other variations as the surf changes.

## Hot stone massage

Treat someone to a hot stone massage. Pick some flat pebbles from the beach that have warmed in the sun and place them along their back. Make sure they are not too hot though! The warmth of the stones is very relaxing.

31

## Wavejumping

Wavejumping is fun and addictive. Stand in the shallows and try and jump clean over every wave. You can play a knockout game in the shallows. You must jump over every wave, first on two legs. If you miss a wave you must try it hopping on one leg. If you touch a wave again, then try two legs but facing the beach, then one leg facing the beach. If you touch the wave again you are out. Who's the best wavejumper?

You can hire surfboards and wetsuits at some beaches, and sometimes arrange for a lesson, too. It's a bit too complicated to cover in this book, but give it a try, it's great fun.

## Snorkelling

If you have a snorkel and mask, then find an area of clear water and see what you can see! Fit the mask strap around the widest part of your head. Breathe in through your nose and it will create a seal. Put the snorkel mouthpiece in your mouth and let your lips rest around it. Practise breathing before you get in the water to get the hang of it. Look up every minute or so to check you are not floating offshore, and are in a safe place to swim. If your mask fills with water, surface and lift the bottom to empty it. If the snorkel fills, blow through the tube to clear it.

## Skimboarding

Skim boards are short, flat egg-shaped boards. Slide the board onto the sand as the surf is going out. Then skim along the shallow receding water. Timing takes practice. Too early and you end up in a pool of water, too late and you get stuck in sand!

## Against the tide

Split into teams and head to the sea with your buckets and spades. Each team needs to build a mound close to the incoming tide. Give yourselves ten minutes to build it. Then stand a team member on top of the mound, and see who can keep their balance the longest as the tide comes in. The last team with their mascot still standing on their team's 'castle', wins.

## Bodyboarding

If there are breaking waves on the beach, bodyboarding is great fun. On many beaches you can hire or buy boards. Only bodyboard if you are a good swimmer, and if there are lifeguards present. Read the beach safety section in this book first to understand about safety and flags. To catch a wave, lie on your board as the wave approaches and start paddling hard with your arms. The wave should catch you and push you along into the shore.

# Beachcombing

**There's so much to see on the beach if you know where to look. Here's a guide to how to do it and what you might find.**

### When to beachcomb?

The best conditions for beach combing are during the winter, early in the morning, as the tide is going out, and right after a storm. It's a bit like a car boot sale, the first people get the best stuff. Storms churn up a lot of rare things. When the tide is going out it leaves fresh finds, but a low tide means there is more sand to search. Bad weather in winter means you may find a spot that hasn't been combed for weeks.

### Where to look?

At the top of the beach you will find a line of debris washed up by the last high tide, called the strandline. This is a good place to beachcomb. Wear gloves and supervise young children.

Anything and everything gets washed up on the shore, sometimes even unexploded wartime bombs! If you're not sure, leave it alone.

# What's That? Guide to Beachcombing

## Egg cases

The smallest egg case you might find is of the common whelk (top). This cluster of egg cases looks like a bathroom sponge. Skates, rays and sharks all produce egg cases known as mermaid's purses (bottom).

## Cuttlefish bone

The cuttlefish is related to the octopus. The bone (left) is the internal shell, made up of small compartments that fill with gas to help it float. It looks a bit like white polystyrene.

## Jellyfish

You can often find washed up jellyfish on the beach. But beware, even dead jellyfish can sting you. Compass jellyfish (right) can have stripes and thin tentacles.

## Starfish

You may be lucky enough to find a starfish. There are over 30 different types of starfish in the UK including brittle stars, cushion stars and sea stars.

## Seaweed

There are 650 species of seaweed around the UK! The commonest seaweeds are the 'wracks'. Bladder wrack (top) and channeled wrack (middle) can be found on the upper and midshore. In rockpools you can find green seaweeds called ulva (bottom right) and red seaweeds called corallina (bottom left).

Take a look at some seaweed. It may have stowaways attached! Bouy barnacles attach themselves to floating objects and go where the tides take them.

## Driftwood

Beaten by waves, pounded by rain and bleached by the sun, driftwood can be beautiful. You can make sculptures or picture frames or sell the driftwood to florists.

## Shells

See what shells you
can find along the beach.
Here are some shells
that you may see.

crab shell

periwinkle

cockle

limpet

razor clam

mussels

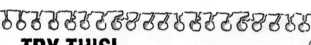

### TRY THIS!

See if you can find some sea glass.
Sea glass has been polished smooth and
rounded over many years by the action
of the wind, the sand and the sea. It is
sometimes called mermaid's tears!

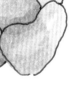

# What's Living in the Sand?

## What's living in the sand?

There are a few creatures living
in the sand under your feet.
Have a look.

## Lugworm

Look for a worm cast on the surface near a small hole or
depression. Between these two is a 'U' shaped burrow with
a lugworm living in it! It eats any food that falls into the
dip and poos sand out the other end every 40-50 minutes.

## Sand-hopper

Sand-hoppers live under the strandline
and eat rotting seaweed. They
generally come out at night and
burrow during the day.

## Weever fish

Weever fish are sandy-coloured and
about six inches long. They hide in
the sand in shallow warm water.
With venomous spines on their backs,
they give a nasty sting so wear flip
flops if they are on your beach.

## Cockles

Cockles live burrowed in the
sand. When the tide is in, they
suck in food through a tube.
Cockles can 'jump' by bending
and straightening their foot!

## Up close sand

Take a small handful of sand home with you, spread it on black paper and take a look. Shell sand is white or yellow and made when waves grind up shells. If sand gives off tiny bubbles when you drop a bit of vinegar on it, that means it was part of something that was once alive, like coral, shells, or bone. Grey sand is usually river sand, made from hard rocks like granite. Cliffs worn by the power of the sea become sand too. Pink beaches usually get their colour from tiny bits of coral and other animals. Small, jewel-like coloured grains are usually bits of broken glass that have been smoothed by the sand and waves.

## Do a litter pick

Help the environment. When you are beachcombing, take a bin bag with you, every little bit helps! Plastic doesn't break down and floats around in our oceans for years. Plastic bags get eaten by turtles. Birds get tangled in beer can holders. Balloons get tangled or get eaten. Fishing lines and nets tangle marine wildlife and they drown. Cigarette ends are often eaten by mistake. Anything you pick up will help save sealife and make the beach nicer. Wear gloves. If you're not sure about something, leave it.

# Rockpooling

**Rockpooling is a great way to spend a few hours on the beach. See what you can find. A bucket and net can be handy.**

### A Typical Rockpool

Exploring a rock pool is great fun. It is best to arrive about four hours after high tide. Turn over rocks gently to see if anything is hiding. Be careful and return the rock to exactly the same position and the same way up as you found it. If you place the rock back upside down, the attached life will die. This picture shows typical rockpool life.

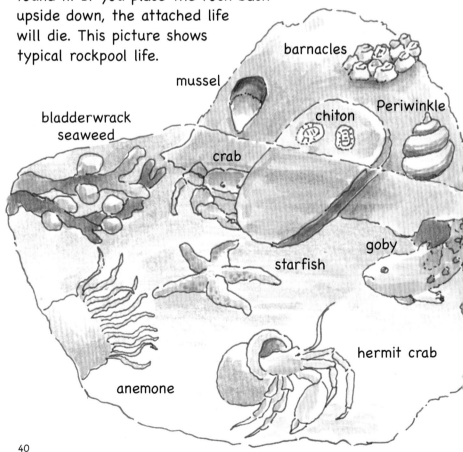

barnacles

mussel

Periwinkle

chiton

bladderwrack seaweed

crab

goby

starfish

hermit crab

anemone

## What can you find?

Common rockpool fish are flatfish, buried in the sand with just their eyes showing: sand eels, gobies and blennies. Gobies often hide under stones. Shrimps like sandy-bottomed pools and prawns rocky-bottomed pools. Crabs hide under seaweed or rocks. Rocks can be covered in barnacles and seaweed. Winkles or periwinkles look a bit like snails. Sea anemones are often stuck to the rocks. Gently brush them with a finger and they will cling to you.

## Some more unusual finds...

There are over 30 different types of starfish in the UK including brittle stars and cushion stars. An unusual jellyfish is the By-the-wind sailor. It is small and usually deep blue in colour, with a small stiff sail that catches the wind and propels them over the surface of the sea. Under certain wind conditions, they can be stranded on beaches in their thousands! These jellyfish are harmless, but generally, don't touch a jellyfish, as most will sting you. The largest jellyfish is the Lion's mane jellyfish and its sting is harmful.

Brittle star

Cushion star

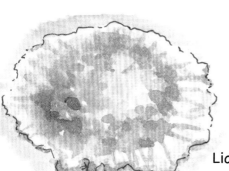

Lion's mane jellyfish

By-the-wind sailor

# Sea wildlife

**Our coasts are home to seals, sharks, dolphins, porpoises and some amazing fish.**

### Seals
Atlantic grey seals have a flat profile with nostrils that are quite far apart. Common seals have a dipped forehead with 'V' shaped nostrils and a shorter snub snout. A common seal's head looks too small for its body.

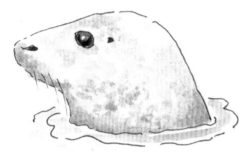

Grey seal

Common seal
(or harbour seal)

### Sunfish
You can sometimes see sunfish when the sea is warm, and their food, jellyfish, is about. It is the heaviest known bony fish in the world. They often swim near the surface, and their fins are sometimes mistaken for sharks. You can tell it's not by the motion of the fin, which swings in a sculling motion.

## Sharks!

There are at least 21 species of shark around the coasts of Britain, from the small-spotted catshark to the large streamlined blue shark and plankton-eating basking shark. At least half of British sharks, including the dogfish, porbeagle and basking shark, are here all year-round.

## Dolphins, whales and porpoises

Keep your eyes peeled out to sea and you may spot harbour porpoises, common dolphins and bottlenose dolphins in inshore areas.

Try mackerel spotting. Shoals can be found around headlands, breakwaters, piers and reefs. Watch for diving birds, lots of jellyfish, or small bubbles breaking at the surface of the water. This effect is seen when mackerel are feeding.

# Fin spotter guide

Basking shark

Porbeagle shark

Dolphin

Harbour porpoise

# Seabirds

A large waterbird, the cormorant is often seen standing with its wings held out to dry.

shag

cormorant

Shags are goose-sized dark long-necked birds similar to cormorants but smaller and generally slimmer with a characteristic steep forehead.

fulmar

The guillemot comes to land only to nest, spending the rest of its life at sea.

guillemot

The Fulmar is a gull-like, grey and white seabird. Its flight behaviour is quite different from gulls though. Stiff-winged glides and quick wing-beats are characteristic of its flight.

# Exploring the cliffs

There is plenty to explore around the beach.
Cliffs can have caves and wildlife of their own.
You can find fossils, too.

## What can you see in a cave?

You can sometimes see bats and seabirds
nesting in tall, dry caves. You can imagine
smugglers and pirates hiding their treasure in
the darkness. On deserted beaches you may
find baby seals sheltering in caves. Seal
mothers leave their pups alone for short
periods of time while they look for food. If
you do see any wildlife, leave the cave. Being
too close causes stress, and a seal could bite.
Adults may even abandon their young.

### Exploring caves

It's fun to explore caves but it can
be very dangerous. Always tell
someone where you are going,
your phone will NOT work! Never
go caving alone. Stay out of a
cave if there is threatening
weather or the tide is coming in.
Caves can flood quickly. Watch
where you are stepping. Avoid
piles of rubble or anything that
looks unstable. Caves can be slippery
and dark. Take a torch with you if
you have one.

## Cliffs

Along many sections of the coast there are footpaths and coastpaths which are great to explore and to get good views of the beach. If you take your binoculars you may see basking sharks, seals and dolphins further out to sea. You could see lizards or snakes basking on stone walls, and find many unusual wild flowers that are only seen by the sea.

lizard

adder

basking shark

You don't have to get on a boat to see a basking shark. Watching from the cliffs is probably the best way to see them. It doesn't disturb the sharks, so they are more likely to stay around for longer.

## Cliff safety

Cliffs can be dangerous, so do not stray off the path, and be especially cautious after any heavy rainfall and frosts as cliff edges are more likely to crumble away. Keep dogs on a lead as many fall off cliffs every year chasing rabbits. Avoid parts of the beach or cliffs where there is fresh rockfall. They often occur repeatedly at the same place.

## Tides

Twice daily the tide comes in, about 50 minutes later than the previous day. Spring tides bring a higher than normal tidal range (the high tide is very high, the low tide is very low). The highest spring tides of the year happen after the equinoxes in March and September. High spring tides are at about the same time of the day every year in each location on the coast! This means that low springs occur at dawn and dusk in Brighton but occur around the middle of the day in south Devon.

## Fossil hunting

Collecting fossils is fun. You could be the first person ever to see them! Fossils form when an animal is buried in mud or sand. Over thousands of years the mud turns into rock. You can usually find fossils where this type of sedimentary rock is exposed at the surface. Only collect what you

need. Some fossils are best left where they are for others to enjoy. Some places are protected by law, so check if you are unsure. Watch out for falling rocks and places you could slip or fall over, and make sure you don't get cut off from the land by the tide coming in. Check the tide times before you start.

# Packing up

**Here are some tips on how to pack up safely and leave the beach as you found it.**

- Bag up your rubbish and bin it or take it home
- Put wet towels and bathing suits in plastic bags
- Cool down your car by covering the windscreen and opening the windows a while before you leave
- Pour water on the barbecue and on the sand where it was until it is cool. Never put hot coal in a bin
- Take all food with you, don't leave it for the gulls as they can become a nuisance if fed
- Check which way the wind is blowing before shaking your towels. Your neighbours don't want a face full of sand!
- Check the sand around where you sat in case anything fell out of your pockets
- Fill in any holes you have dug, or rock piles you have made
- Don't take pebbles or sand from the beach. This causes beach erosion and is illegal. Leave everything where it is for others to enjoy